LIVE
LAUGH
LOVE

summersdale

LIVE, LAUGH, LOVE

Summersdale Publishers Ltd
46 West Street
Chichester
West Sussex
PO19 1RP
UK

www.summersdale.com

Printed and bound in the Czech Republic

ISBN: 978-1-84953-528-1

Substantial discounts on bulk quantities of Summersdale books are available to corporations, professional associations and other organisations. For details contact Nicky Douglas by telephone: +44 (0) 1243 756902, fax: +44 (0) 1243 786300 or email: nicky@summersdale.com.

TO...

FROM...

ONE CANNOT HAVE TOO LARGE A PARTY.

Jane Austen

LAUGHTER IS AN INSTANT VACATION.

Milton Berle

ALL THE STATISTICS
IN THE WORLD CAN'T
MEASURE THE WARMTH
OF A SMILE.

Chris Hart

MIX A LITTLE
FOOLISHNESS WITH YOUR
SERIOUS PLANS. IT IS
LOVELY TO BE SILLY AT
THE RIGHT MOMENT.

Horace

PLUNGE BOLDLY INTO
THE THICK OF LIFE,
AND SEIZE IT WHERE
YOU WILL, IT IS ALWAYS
INTERESTING.

Johann Wolfgang von Goethe

LOVE IS BEING STUPID TOGETHER.

Paul Valéry

DARE TO LOVE YOURSELF
AS IF YOU WERE A
RAINBOW WITH GOLD AT
BOTH ENDS.

Aberjhani

LAUGHTER IS THE SOUND OF THE SOUL DANCING.

Jarod Kintz

LOVE ALL, TRUST A FEW, DO WRONG TO NONE.

William Shakespeare

EVERY DAY BRINGS
A CHANCE FOR YOU
TO DRAW IN A BREATH,
KICK OFF YOUR SHOES...
AND DANCE.

Oprah Winfrey

LIFE IS A GREAT BIG
CANVAS, AND YOU
SHOULD THROW ALL THE
PAINT ON IT YOU CAN.

Danny Kaye

DON'T GO THROUGH LIFE, GROW THROUGH LIFE.

Eric Butterworth

LAUGHTER IS THE
BRUSH THAT SWEEPS
AWAY THE COBWEBS OF
YOUR HEART.

Mort Walker

OPPORTUNITIES DON'T
OFTEN COME ALONG.
SO, WHEN THEY DO, YOU
HAVE TO GRAB THEM.

Audrey Hepburn

WHERE THERE IS GREAT LOVE THERE ARE ALWAYS MIRACLES.

Willa Cather

LAUGHTER IS A TRANQUILISER WITH NO SIDE EFFECTS.

Arnold H. Glasow

TOO MUCH OF A GOOD THING CAN BE WONDERFUL.

Mae West

IF YOU GIVE PEOPLE A
CHANCE, THEY SHINE.

Billy Connolly

THE GOOD LIFE IS ONE
INSPIRED BY LOVE AND
GUIDED BY KNOWLEDGE.

Bertrand Russell

FIND SOMETHING YOU'RE PASSIONATE ABOUT AND KEEP TREMENDOUSLY INTERESTED IN IT.

Julia Child

WHOEVER IS HAPPY WILL MAKE OTHERS HAPPY TOO.

Anne Frank

IN THE ARITHMETIC OF
LOVE, ONE PLUS ONE
EQUALS EVERYTHING,
AND TWO MINUS ONE
EQUALS NOTHING.

Mignon McLaughlin

IT IS MORE FUN TO
BE THE PAINTER THAN
THE PAINT.

George Clooney

WHERE THERE IS LOVE
THERE IS LIFE.

Mahatma Gandhi

TRUE HAPPINESS
COMES FROM THE JOY
OF DEEDS WELL DONE,
THE ZEST OF CREATING
THINGS NEW.

Antoine de Saint-Exupéry

BE YOURSELF.
THE WORLD WORSHIPS
THE ORIGINAL.

Ingrid Bergman

CARRY LAUGHTER WITH YOU WHEREVER YOU GO.

Hugh Sidey

HE HAS ACHIEVED
SUCCESS WHO HAS LIVED
WELL, LAUGHED OFTEN,
AND LOVED MUCH.

Bessie Anderson Stanley

'TIS BETTER TO HAVE
LOVED AND LOST
THAN NEVER TO HAVE
LOVED AT ALL.

Alfred, Lord Tennyson

I THINK THAT BEAUTY
COMES FROM BEING
HAPPY AND CONNECTED
TO THE PEOPLE WE LOVE.

Marcia Cross

THE LIMITS OF
THE POSSIBLE CAN ONLY
BE DEFINED BY GOING
BEYOND THEM INTO
THE IMPOSSIBLE.

Arthur C. Clarke

DO YOUR LITTLE BIT
OF GOOD WHERE
YOU ARE; IT'S THOSE
LITTLE BITS OF GOOD
PUT TOGETHER THAT
OVERWHELM THE WORLD.

Desmond Tutu

ESKIMOS HAD FIFTY-
TWO NAMES FOR
SNOW BECAUSE IT WAS
IMPORTANT TO THEM;
THERE OUGHT TO BE AS
MANY FOR LOVE.

Margaret Atwood

DO NOT DWELL IN THE PAST, DO NOT DREAM OF THE FUTURE, CONCENTRATE THE MIND ON THE PRESENT MOMENT.

Siddhārtha Gautama Buddha

THE HUMAN RACE HAS
ONLY ONE REALLY
EFFECTIVE WEAPON AND
THAT IS LAUGHTER.

Mark Twain

THROW CAUTION TO THE WIND AND JUST DO IT.

Carrie Underwood

LOVE IS THE MAGICIAN THAT PULLS MAN OUT OF HIS OWN HAT.

Ben Hecht

WHEREVER YOU GO, GO WITH ALL YOUR HEART.

Confucius

FOLLOW YOUR OWN STAR.

Dante Alighieri

LAUGHTER IS THE
SHORTEST DISTANCE
BETWEEN TWO PEOPLE.

Victor Borge

YOU CAN, YOU SHOULD,
AND IF YOU'RE BRAVE
ENOUGH TO START,
YOU WILL.

Stephen King

WHEN YOU'RE TRUE TO WHO YOU ARE, AMAZING THINGS HAPPEN.

Deborah Norville

WHAT DOES LOVE FEEL LIKE? INCREDIBLE.

Rebecca Adlington

IF YOU'RE GOING TO BE
THINKING ANYTHING,
YOU MIGHT AS WELL
THINK BIG.

Donald Trump

LOVE IS THE ENCHANTED DAWN OF EVERY HEART.

Alphonse de Lamartine

I'D FAR RATHER BE HAPPY THAN RIGHT ANY DAY.

Douglas Adams

OUR SOULMATE IS THE
ONE WHO MAKES LIFE
COME TO LIFE.

Richard Bach

LAUGH AND THE WORLD LAUGHS WITH YOU.

Ella Wheeler Wilcox

WE CAN ONLY LEARN TO LOVE BY LOVING.

Iris Murdoch

LIFE IS A HELLUVA LOT
MORE FUN IF YOU SAY
'YES' RATHER THAN 'NO'.

Richard Branson

LOVE IS EVERYTHING
IT'S CRACKED UP TO BE...
IT REALLY IS WORTH
FIGHTING FOR, BEING
BRAVE FOR, RISKING
EVERYTHING FOR.

Erica Jong

LOSE NOT YOURSELF IN
A FAR OFF TIME, SEIZE
THE MOMENT THAT
IS THINE.

Friedrich Schiller

LIFE IS THE FLOWER
FOR WHICH LOVE IS
THE HONEY.

Victor Hugo

IN DREAMS AND IN
LOVE THERE ARE NO
IMPOSSIBILITIES.

János Arany

YOU NEVER LOSE
BY LOVING.

Barbara De Angelis

WHY NOT JUST LIVE
IN THE MOMENT,
ESPECIALLY IF IT HAS A
GOOD BEAT?

Goldie Hawn

EVERYTHING IN OUR LIFE SHOULD BE BASED ON LOVE.

Ray Bradbury

TO THINE OWN SELF
BE TRUE.

William Shakespeare

THINK BIG THOUGHTS BUT RELISH SMALL PLEASURES.

H. Jackson Brown Jr

WHAT THE WORLD
REALLY NEEDS IS
MORE LOVE AND LESS
PAPERWORK.

Pearl Bailey

THE THING TO DO IS ENJOY THE RIDE WHILE YOU'RE ON IT.

Johnny Depp

THE BEST THING TO HOLD ON TO IN LIFE IS EACH OTHER.

Audrey Hepburn

YOU ONLY GET ONE CHANCE AT LIFE AND YOU HAVE TO GRAB IT BOLDLY.

Bear Grylls

LOVE, IT IS SAID, IS BLIND, BUT LOVE IS NOT BLIND. IT IS AN EXTRA EYE, WHICH SHOWS US WHAT IS MOST WORTHY OF REGARD.

J. M. Barrie

WHY DID WE WAIT FOR
ANY THING? — WHY NOT
SEIZE THE PLEASURE
AT ONCE?

Jane Austen

LIVE SIMPLY. DREAM
BIG. BE GRATEFUL. GIVE
LOVE. LAUGH LOTS.

Anonymous

AT THE HEIGHT OF
LAUGHTER, THE
UNIVERSE IS FLUNG
INTO A KALEIDOSCOPE OF
NEW POSSIBILITIES.

Jean Houston

INTO THE HOUSE WHERE
JOY LIVES, HAPPINESS
WILL GLADLY COME.

Japanese proverb

GO AFTER YOUR DREAMS,
DON'T BE AFRAID TO
PUSH THE BOUNDARIES.
AND LAUGH A LOT — IT'S
GOOD FOR YOU!

Paula Radcliffe

THERE IS NO INSTINCT
LIKE THE HEART.

Lord Byron

A HEART THAT LOVES IS ALWAYS YOUNG.

Greek proverb

YOU LIVE BUT ONCE; YOU MIGHT AS WELL BE AMUSING.

Coco Chanel

IF MY MIND CAN
CONCEIVE IT, AND MY
HEART CAN BELIEVE IT, I
KNOW I CAN ACHIEVE IT.

Jesse Jackson

THE LOVE WE GIVE
AWAY IS THE ONLY
LOVE WE KEEP.

Elbert Hubbard

NOTHING SHOWS A MAN'S CHARACTER MORE THAN WHAT HE LAUGHS AT.

Johann Wolfgang von Goethe

LOVE IS COMPOSED
OF A SINGLE SOUL
INHABITING TWO BODIES.

Aristotle

BE FAITHFUL TO THAT WHICH EXISTS WITHIN YOURSELF.

André Gide

A GOOD LAUGH IS SUNSHINE IN A HOUSE.

William Makepeace Thackeray

MAY YOU LIVE EVERY DAY OF YOUR LIFE.

Jonathan Swift

WHAT FORCE IS MORE POTENT THAN LOVE?

Igor Stravinsky

ENTHUSIASM MOVES THE WORLD.

Arthur Balfour

ALWAYS BE A FIRST-RATE
VERSION OF YOURSELF,
INSTEAD OF A SECOND-
RATE VERSION OF
SOMEBODY ELSE.

Judy Garland

LOVE IS LIKE SMILING; IT NEVER FADES AND IS CONTAGIOUS.

Anonymous

SEE EVERYTHING,
OVERLOOK A GREAT
DEAL, CORRECT A LITTLE.

Pope John XXIII

LOVE IS A CANVAS
FURNISHED BY NATURE
AND EMBROIDERED BY
IMAGINATION.

Voltaire

THERE ARE NO TRAFFIC JAMS ALONG THE EXTRA MILE.

Roger Staubach

TO LOVE AND BE LOVED
IS TO FEEL THE SUN
FROM BOTH SIDES.

David Viscott

DREAM AS IF YOU'LL LIVE FOREVER. LIVE AS IF YOU'LL DIE TODAY.

James Dean

DWELL ON THE BEAUTY
OF LIFE. WATCH
THE STARS, AND SEE
YOURSELF RUNNING
WITH THEM.

Marcus Aurelius

HAPPINESS IS A WAY OF TRAVEL, NOT A DESTINATION.

Roy M. Goodman

IF WE ALL DID THE THINGS WE ARE CAPABLE OF, WE WOULD ASTOUND OURSELVES.

Thomas Edison

FIRST SAY TO YOURSELF
WHAT YOU WOULD BE;
AND THEN DO WHAT YOU
HAVE TO DO.

Epictetus

THE FUTURE DEPENDS
ON WHAT YOU DO TODAY.

Mahatma Gandhi

HAVE A HEART THAT
NEVER HARDENS, AND
A TEMPER THAT NEVER
TIRES, AND A TOUCH
THAT NEVER HURTS.

Charles Dickens

LAUGHTER TO ME IS
BEING ALIVE.

William Saroyan

IT IS NEVER TOO LATE
TO BE WHAT YOU MIGHT
HAVE BEEN.

George Eliot

THE PURPOSE
OF DANCING — AND OF
LIFE — IS TO ENJOY
EVERY MOMENT AND
EVERY STEP.

Wayne W. Dyer

TELL ME WHO ADMIRES AND LOVES YOU AND I WILL TELL YOU WHO YOU ARE.

Charles-Augustin Sainte-Beuve

THE GREATEST PLEASURE OF LIFE IS LOVE.

Sir William Temple

BE YOURSELF; EVERYONE ELSE IS ALREADY TAKEN.

Oscar Wilde

NOTHING TO ME FEELS AS GOOD AS LAUGHING INCREDIBLY HARD.

Steve Carell

LIFE IS SHORT.
KISS SLOWLY, LAUGH
INSANELY, LOVE TRULY
AND FORGIVE QUICKLY.

Paulo Coelho

WRINKLES SHOULD
MERELY INDICATE
WHERE THE SMILES
HAVE BEEN.

Mark Twain

LOVE IS LIKE PI —
NATURAL, IRRATIONAL,
AND VERY IMPORTANT.

Lisa Hoffman

DON'T COUNT THE DAYS; MAKE THE DAYS COUNT.

Anonymous

THE ONLY REASON TO BE ALIVE IS TO ENJOY IT.

Rita Mae Brown

LOVE IS A GAME
THAT TWO CAN PLAY
AND BOTH WIN.

Eva Gabor

ACT AS IF WHAT YOU DO MAKES A DIFFERENCE. IT DOES.

William James

IF YOU HAVE GOOD
THOUGHTS THEY WILL
SHINE OUT OF YOUR
FACE LIKE SUNBEAMS
AND YOU WILL ALWAYS
LOOK LOVELY.

Roald Dahl

LOVE IS THE BEE
THAT CARRIES THE
POLLEN FROM ONE
HEART TO ANOTHER.

Slash Coleman

WE BUILD TOO
MANY WALLS AND NOT
ENOUGH BRIDGES.

Isaac Newton

ENJOY THE LITTLE
THINGS, FOR ONE DAY
YOU MAY LOOK BACK AND
REALISE THEY WERE
THE BIG THINGS.

Robert Brault

DON'T WAIT. THE TIME WILL NEVER BE JUST RIGHT.

Napoleon Hill

I HONESTLY THINK IT'S
THE THING I LIKE MOST,
TO LAUGH. IT CURES A
MULTITUDE OF ILLS.

Audrey Hepburn

LIFE IS NOT MEASURED
BY THE NUMBER OF
BREATHS YOU TAKE, BUT
BY THE MOMENTS THAT
TAKE YOUR BREATH
AWAY.

Anonymous

LOVE LOVES TO LOVE LOVE.

James Joyce

TRY TO BE LIKE THE
TURTLE — AT EASE IN
YOUR OWN SHELL.

Bill Copeland

DO SOMETHING WONDERFUL, PEOPLE MAY IMITATE IT.

Albert Schweitzer

THERE IS ONLY ONE
HAPPINESS IN LIFE: TO
LOVE AND BE LOVED.

George Sand

THERE IS NOTHING
IN THE WORLD SO
IRRESISTIBLY CONTAGIOUS
AS LAUGHTER AND
GOOD HUMOUR.

Charles Dickens

ALWAYS DO WHAT IS
RIGHT. IT WILL GRATIFY
HALF OF MANKIND AND
ASTOUND THE OTHER.

Mark Twain

THE THINGS THAT WE LOVE TELL US WHAT WE ARE.

Thomas Aquinas

ALWAYS LAUGH
WHEN YOU CAN. IT IS
CHEAP MEDICINE.

Lord Byron

EVERY MOMENT IS A
FRESH BEGINNING.

T. S. Eliot

THE MAN THAT LOVES
AND LAUGHS MUST
SURE DO WELL.

Alexander Pope

LEAVE SOMETHING FOR SOMEONE BUT DON'T LEAVE SOMEONE FOR SOMETHING.

Enid Blyton

GIVE OUT WHAT YOU MOST WANT TO COME BACK.

Robin Sharma

GO AS FAR AS YOU CAN
SEE; WHEN YOU GET
THERE, YOU'LL BE ABLE
TO SEE FURTHER.

Thomas Carlyle

I AM THANKFUL FOR
LAUGHTER, EXCEPT
WHEN MILK COMES OUT
OF MY NOSE.

Woody Allen

THE MADNESS OF LOVE
IS THE GREATEST OF
HEAVEN'S BLESSINGS.

Plato

WHATEVER YOU ARE, BE A GOOD ONE.

Abraham Lincoln

DON'T SAVE THINGS FOR
A SPECIAL OCCASION.
EVERY DAY OF YOUR LIFE
IS A SPECIAL OCCASION.

Anonymous

WHO, BEING LOVED, IS POOR?

Oscar Wilde

WHATEVER YOU CAN
DO OR DREAM YOU CAN,
BEGIN IT. BOLDNESS HAS
GENIUS, POWER AND
MAGIC IN IT.

Johann Wolfgang von Goethe

LOVE CONQUERS ALL.

Virgil

IF YOU LOVE LIFE, LIFE WILL LOVE YOU BACK.

Arthur Rubinstein

DO ANYTHING, BUT LET IT PRODUCE JOY.

Henry Miller

BEING DEEPLY LOVED
BY SOMEONE GIVES
YOU STRENGTH, WHILE
LOVING SOMEONE DEEPLY
GIVES YOU COURAGE.

Lao Tzu

BEGIN, BE BOLD AND VENTURE TO BE WISE.

Horace

DO NOT WAIT TO STRIKE
TILL THE IRON IS HOT;
BUT MAKE IT HOT
BY STRIKING.

W. B. Yeats

IF YOU ARE EVER IN
DOUBT AS TO WHETHER
OR NOT YOU SHOULD KISS
A PRETTY GIRL, ALWAYS
GIVE HER THE BENEFIT
OF THE DOUBT.

Thomas Carlyle

TO LOVE IS
TO RECEIVE A
GLIMPSE OF
HEAVEN.

Karen Sunde

SOMETIMES THE HEART SEES WHAT IS INVISIBLE TO THE EYE.

H. Jackson Brown Jr

THE MOST WASTED
OF ALL DAYS IS THAT
IN WHICH WE HAVE
NOT LAUGHED.

Nicolas Chamfort

THE IMPORTANT
THING... IS NOT HOW
MANY YEARS IN YOUR
LIFE, BUT HOW MUCH
LIFE IN YOUR YEARS!

Edward Stieglitz

TRUE LOVE STORIES NEVER HAVE ENDINGS.

Richard Bach

BE HAPPY WITH WHAT
YOU HAVE AND ARE, BE
GENEROUS WITH BOTH,
AND YOU WON'T HAVE TO
HUNT FOR HAPPINESS.

William E. Gladstone

THE MORE WE DO, THE MORE WE CAN DO.

William Hazlitt

THOSE WHO BRING
SUNSHINE INTO THE
LIVES OF OTHERS
CANNOT KEEP IT FROM
THEMSELVES.

J. M. Barrie

WHAT SOAP IS TO THE BODY, LAUGHTER IS TO THE SOUL.

Yiddish proverb

WHEN YOU COME TO A FORK IN THE ROAD, TAKE IT.

Yogi Berra

I THINK TO LOVE
BRAVELY IS THE BEST.

Marilyn Monroe

RISE TO THE OCCASION, WHICH IS LIFE.

Virginia Euwer Wolff

IF OPPORTUNITY DOESN'T KNOCK, BUILD A DOOR.

Milton Berle

LAUGHTER IS A
SUNBEAM OF THE SOUL.

Thomas Mann

DO ALL THINGS
WITH LOVE.

Og Mandino

@EsmeTheBird

If you're interested in finding out more about our books, find us on Facebook at **Summersdale Publishers** and follow us on Twitter at **@Summersdale**.

www.summersdale.com